Small Pet Care

CARING FOR RABBITS, HAMSTERS AND GUINEA PIGS

Small Pet Care

Caring for Rabbits, Hamsters and Guinea Pigs

Annabel Blackledge

DK

LONDON, NEW YORK, MUNICH, MELBOURNE AND DELHI

FOR BOOKWORK LTD:
WRITTEN AND EDITED BY Annabel Blackledge
SENIOR ART EDITOR Kate Mullins
CONSULTANT Victoria Cyphus BVetMed MRCVS

SPECIAL PHOTOGRAPHY Steven Teague

FOR DORLING KINDERSLEY:
ORIGINAL SERIES STYLING Lisa Lanzarini
DTP DESIGNER Lauren Egan
PUBLISHING MANAGERS Cynthia O'Neill
and Simon Beecroft
ART DIRECTOR Mark Richards
CATEGORY PUBLISHER Alex Kirkham
PRODUCTION Alison Lenane

First published in Great Britain in 2005
by Dorling Kindersley Limited
80 Strand, London WC2R 0RL
A Penguin Company

05 06 07 08 09 10 9 8 7 6 5 4 3 2 1

The publisher would like to thank the following for their
kind permission to reproduce their photographs:

(Key: a-above; c-centre; b-below; l-left; r-right; t-top)

Ardea London Ltd: Elizabeth Bomford 6cr

All other images © Dorling Kindersley Picture Library:

7c, 20tl, 44tl Paul Bricknall: 22tl, 22cb, 22br, 23cb, 23br, 23bl, 23br,
26tl, 28tl, 30tl, 32c, 33tl, 34c 39br, 40tl, 42cr 44bl. Jane Burton: 7tr, 7ct,
Andy Crawford: 37tr. Mike Dunning: 39cl. Steve Shott: 8tl, 8cl, 8c, 8cr,
15tr, 16tl. Kim Taylor: 30br. Steve Teague: 1, 2-3, 4-5, 6tl, 6bl, 7tl, 7bl,
8cr, 9r, 10-11, 12-13, 14tl, 14br, 15c, 15cl, 15br, 16cl, 16br, 17l, 17tr,
17cr, 17br, 18-19, 20b, 21tl, 21cl, 21bl, 21tr, 21cr, 21cb, 22c, 23tl, 24-25,
26l, 26cr, 27tl, 27tc, 27br, 28cr, 28b, 29tl, 29b, 30l, 30cr, 31cl, 31bl, 31r,
32tl, 32cr, 32bl, 32br, 33b, 34br, 35bl, 35r, 35br, 36l, 36c, 37b, 38l, 39tr,
40c, 40bl, 41, 42tl, 42c, 42bl, 42br, 43, 44cr, 45l, 45tr, 46-47, 48bl.
Barrie Watts: 9tl.
Jacket: Paul Bricknall: br. Barnabus Kindersley: bcl. Steve Teague: front,
bl, bcr, back.

A CIP catalogue record for this book
is available from the British Library.

ISBN 1-4053-0822-2

Reproduced by Colourscan, Singapore
Printed and bound at L.E.G.O. Italy

Discover more at
www.dk.com

NOTE TO PARENTS This book teaches children how to be caring, responsible small-pet owners. However, your child will need help and support from you or a professional in all aspects of their pet's care. Don't let your child have a pet unless you are certain that your family has the time and resources to look after it for its entire life.
When you see the sign "!" in a purple circle, you should take special note.
NOTE TO CHILDREN In this book we say *either* "he" *or* "she" when we talk about how to look after your small pet. This changes depending on whether the animal in the photo is a boy or a girl, but the advice we give applies to small pets of both sexes.

Contents

Which pet?

FROM RABBITS TO rats, gerbils to guinea pigs, there are all sorts of small pets available. Some need to live indoors and some need to spend time outdoors. Some need companions and some prefer to live alone. Whichever small pet you choose, you will need to find the time every day to feed her, groom her, keep her home clean and make sure that she is happy and healthy.

Rabbits and guinea pigs do not make good companions. Rabbits tend to be too rough, which can result in guinea pigs getting scared or injured.

If you give your rabbit lots of love and attention, he will soon become part of the family.

Rabbits

Rabbits are sociable, inquisitive and love to be petted. If you've got room for a large hutch and have a grassy garden, a rabbit could be the perfect pet for you. They are quite easy to house-train, and a happy "house rabbit" will follow you around everywhere, hoping for treats and fuss. Rabbits need company so, ideally, it is best to choose two or more from the same litter.

THINK FIRST

- Can you afford a pet? Food and bedding materials are quite cheap, but vet bills, hutches and cages can be expensive.
- Do you have time? You will need to see to your pet's needs and play with her every day.
- Do you have space? Your pet will need a home and a place to play and exercise.
- Is your family prepared? You will need help and support.

OTHER SMALL PETS

Rabbits, hamsters and guinea pigs are some of the most popular small pets, but there are lots of others to choose from, too. Find out as much as possible about how to care for the small animal you decide on before you bring it home.

Chipmunks

These curious, squirrel-like animals love climbing and chasing each other. They are great fun to watch.

Gerbils

These animals love to play and burrow, and can grow quite tame with regular handling.

Rats and mice

These animals look similar, but their needs are different. Rats are intelligent, and need a lot of space and attention. Mice are smaller, livelier and harder to handle.

Hamsters

Hamsters live indoors, so they are ideal pets if you don't have a garden. If you choose a hamster, you will need to make time to feed, handle and care for her every evening. It is best not to disturb hamsters in the day because they are nocturnal.

Guinea pigs are usually very gentle – it is extremely rare for them to bite or scratch.

Guinea pigs

Like rabbits, guinea pigs need a large hutch and a grassy outdoor area. Ideally, they also need the company of other guinea pigs. They make rewarding pets – they tend to be easier to handle than rabbits, and are fun to watch as they go about their business, squeaking and grunting happily.

Choosing a rabbit

BEFORE YOU CHOOSE a rabbit, think hard about which type would suit you best. They come in all shapes and sizes, and all have different needs and characters. Make sure that the rabbit you choose has been well cared for. If he has dry bedding, clean drinking water and fresh food it probably means that he has had a healthy start in life.

Rabbits need company and like to live in pairs or small groups. A single rabbit may get lonely and moody.

English Lop rabbit

WHERE TO LOOK

Rabbits are available from rescue centres, private breeders and pet shops. You can try looking in a local newspaper for information about nearby rescue centres and breeders with rabbits for sale.

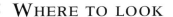

Dutch rabbits

Netherland Dwarf rabbit

Gentle giants

The English Lop has the largest ears in the rabbit world, but the Flemish Giant is the biggest rabbit, weighing about 7 kg (15 lb). Large rabbits make great pets because they tend to be calm and gentle.

Happy medium

Medium-sized rabbits like the Dutch are popular. They are usually good-natured and their size makes them easy to handle. They don't eat as much as their larger relatives and need a bit less living space.

Little ones

The Netherland Dwarf is the smallest breed of pet rabbit, weighing less than 1 kg (2 lb). Small rabbits can be nervous and shy, and do not make ideal pets for first-time rabbit owners.

Furry friend

Long-haired rabbits like the Cashmere Lop and the Angora look irresistibly cuddly. But if you choose a long-haired rabbit, she will need daily grooming to keep her fluffy coat healthy.

Cashmere Lop rabbit

How to spot a healthy rabbit

A healthy rabbit will have clean, bright eyes, a clean nose and mouth, clean ears and a clean bottom. He should have a soft, smooth coat and should be happy to be stroked and picked up. Choose a rabbit that seems inquisitive and playful rather than one that is hiding in a corner.

Dwarf Lops are medium-sized and they make excellent pets. They tend to be friendly and love to be petted – a gentle rub between the ears will probably go down particularly well!

! Ideally, your rabbit will need a safe outside space where he can exercise and nibble on grass.

BASIC ESSENTIALS

Carrying box with removable lid

Wood-based litter and tray

Dust-free wood shavings

Dust-free hay

Dust-free straw

Cleaning materials

Grooming kit

Water bottle

Food and bowl

Getting ready

BEFORE YOU BRING your rabbit home, you will need to get some basic supplies, such as a hutch for her to sleep in, an enclosure for her to play in, a carrying box, bedding and food. You can get extras like toys later. Bunny-proof your home and garden by moving harmful plants, protecting electric cables and putting valuables and breakables out of reach.

!

Place the hutch in a sheltered spot. Rabbits don't like to get too hot or too cold.

Outdoor life

If your rabbit is going to live mainly outside, he will need a sturdy wooden hutch with a rain-proof roof, a cosy nest compartment and a living area with a wire door. A hutch for two medium-sized rabbits needs to be at least 150 cm (60 in) wide, 60 cm (24 in) tall and 60 cm (24 in) deep.

An indoor hutch with a plastic base is best.

A hutch that is raised off the ground is less likely to get damp inside in wet weather.

Sloping rain-proof roof with overhang at front

Inside story

As long as your rabbit gets to play outside regularly, he can live indoors. Keep the hutch in a room where he will get lots of attention, but provide a nest box so that he can hide away if he wants to.

Room to run

Your rabbit will need an enclosure or run where she can hop around and eat grass. It should be as large as possible with an area where she can shelter from sun and rain. If your rabbit likes to dig, you will need to get an enclosure with a wire base.

Let your rabbit come out of the box or hutch in her own time. You can try to tempt her out, but don't reach in and grab her.

Making friends

WHEN YOUR RABBIT first arrives home, he will probably be nervous and shy. But if you are patient and gentle, it won't be long before you are the best of friends. Give your rabbit time to settle in before introducing him to your friends or other members of the family. If you already have a rabbit at home, ask your vet for some advice before introducing them.

Building trust

Your rabbit will soon grow to trust you, especially if you are patient and wait for him to come to you. Try lying on the floor and reading a book while he hops around the room. In time, curiosity will get the better of him and he will come to investigate you. Let him sniff you, and pet him gently without trying to pick him up.

Your rabbit will find you less threatening if you sit or lie down near him.

TRAINING TIPS

- Litter-train your rabbit. Place a tray where he goes to the toilet and reward him with a treat if he uses it.

- Never smack your rabbit.

- Teach your rabbit to come when you call him. If you give him a treat every time he comes, he will learn extremely quickly.

- Never chase your rabbit. Coax him gently until he does what you want him to.

! Rabbits have very sharp claws and may sometimes scratch you by mistake.

Hold tight

Rabbits are strong, but their bones are fragile, so it is important that you hold your rabbit correctly. Pick him up by slipping one hand under his bottom and the other under his chest. Hold him firmly but gently, and close to your body so he doesn't panic and struggle. Always support his bottom.

Put your rabbit down back legs first to prevent either of you getting hurt.

Make sure your rabbit has unlimited fresh hay. It is essential for his digestion and good for his teeth. Nibbling will also help to prevent him from getting bored.

Feeding

YOUR RABBIT'S DIET should be as close as possible to that of a wild rabbit. Hay and grass should make up the bulk of what she eats, with pellets, fresh vegetables and the occasional treat as supplements. Make feeding time as interesting as possible. Offer her a variety of vegetables, and try hiding them around her hutch for her to find.

Eating habits

Rabbits are grazers, which means that they like to eat little and often. Weigh your rabbit and check the pellet packet to find out how much he needs each day, or ask the vet for some advice. It is important to make sure that your rabbit has access to food at all times. If he has eaten his pellets, make sure he has plenty of grass or hay.

(!)

Don't overfeed your rabbit. If he gets fat, he may find it hard to groom himself.

HARMFUL PLANTS

- Potato plants
- Apple seeds (the fruit is safe)
- Rhubarb leaves and stalks
- Buttercups
- Oak leaves and acorns
- Ivy leaves and stalks
- Tomato leaves and stalks (the fruit is safe)

FEEDING RULES

- Try to feed your rabbit at the same times every day.

- Make changes to your rabbit's diet gradually to avoid upsetting his tummy.

- Wash and dry all fruit and vegetables before you feed them to your rabbit.

- Never feed him lawn clippings or anything frozen.

- Clean your rabbit's bowl and water bottle daily, making sure you rinse off any soap.

- Don't let your rabbit graze where insecticides or weed killers have been used.

- Never stop your rabbit from eating his own droppings – it helps him to digest his food.

Drinking water

Whether your rabbit is in her hutch, in her run or running free in the house or garden, she must always have access to clean, fresh drinking water. A drip-feed bottle is best in her hutch because she won't be able to knock it over or make it dirty with food or bedding.

LITTLE TREATS

Most rabbits love treats such as raisins, slices of fruit and stale crusts of wholemeal bread. Offering treats is a great way to win your rabbit's affection and to reward him when he has behaved well. Don't feed him too many though – he may get an upset tummy, become overweight or stop eating his proper food.

Grass and plants

Rabbit pellets

Daily diet

Give your rabbit a bowl of pellets first thing every morning. In the early evenings – before it gets dark – offer him some fresh vegetables. A handful of raw cabbage or a piece of celery should be plenty. If possible, your rabbit also needs to be free to graze on grass and plants such as dandelions and clover for a few hours each day.

Fresh fruit and vegetables

Rabbits are very clean. They spend a lot of time grooming themselves.

Keeping clean

TO KEEP YOUR rabbit happy and healthy, you will need to clean out his hutch every day, groom him regularly and sometimes bath him. Your rabbit may get ill if he has to live in a wet or dirty hutch, or if you do not care properly for his coat. Set aside some time every day to keep your rabbit and his home clean.

Brush

Towel

Comb

Shampoo

GROOMING KIT

To keep your rabbit's coat healthy, you will need a soft brush for everyday grooming, a comb for long-haired rabbits and for removing tangles, some rabbit shampoo and a towel.

Grooming your rabbit

Groom your rabbit at least once a week. If he has long hair or is moulting (in spring and autumn), he will need grooming daily. Brush him carefully all over, raising his front legs to reach his tummy. Grooming helps to remove loose fur, which can cause blockages in your rabbit's stomach if he swallows it as he grooms himself. It is also a great way to bond with him and check that his skin is healthy.

Bath time

Check your rabbit's bottom every day. If it looks dirty, then you may need to wash or bath her to prevent flies laying eggs in the dirt and making her ill. Always ask an adult to help you, and make sure that your rabbit is completely dry before you put her back in her hutch.

Cleaning out

How often your rabbit's hutch needs cleaning will depend on how much time she spends in it. Empty her litter tray and change any wet or dirty bedding daily. The hutch will need a full clean-out at least once a week.

Brush gently in the direction of the fur growth.

1 Take your rabbit out of her hutch and put her somewhere safe. Scoop out all the dirty shavings and straw and any uneaten hay or food.

2 Scrape well into the corners and remove any droppings stuck to the floor. Spray the empty hutch with pet-safe disinfectant every few weeks.

3 Line the floor with clean shavings and put a large pile of straw in the nest compartment. Replace your rabbit's food, hay, litter and water, then put her back in her clean hutch.

Happy rabbit

YOUR RABBIT SHOULD spend as much time as possible out of her hutch every day to exercise and graze. She will also need company, and will be sad if she is shut away too much. The more time you spend playing with your rabbit and watching her go about her business, the better you will get to know her. You will notice straight away if something is wrong.

Rabbits show affection for their companions by snuggling up close and grooming them.

Your rabbit will sit up on her back legs if she's curious and wants to see what's going on around her.

Rabbit language

You can tell a lot about how your rabbit is feeling by observing her behaviour and body language. A happy rabbit will be inquisitive and playful, and when she is tired she might lie down with her legs stretched right out. If your rabbit is unwell, she will probably be quiet and sit hunched up in a corner. If she is angry or alarmed, she might thump her back feet.

RABBIT TOYS

Tunnel

Treat ball

Willow ball

Wood chew

Rope chew

A bonded pair of rabbits will keep each other company when you are not around.

Playtime

Rabbits love to dig, chew, toss and head-butt things. You can buy special toys from pet shops, but most rabbits are happy to dig in a box of hay or tear up an old newspaper. Your rabbit is less likely to get bored in her hutch if she has something to play with. And she is less likely to misbehave when she is out playing if you distract her with things that she is allowed to destroy!

If your rabbit is playing indoors, keep her away from electric cables. If she nibbles one, she could get electrocuted.

Young rabbits need special care. Ask the vet for advice on feeding and weight gain.

Healthcare

YOUR RABBIT'S HEALTH is your responsibility, and there is a lot you can do to help him live a long and healthy life. Take your new rabbit for a health check with a small-animal vet as soon as possible. He should live for up to about eight years, and his needs will vary as he grows up, so be prepared to adapt his care.

The vet will check whether your rabbit is female or male and will advise you about neutering. Neutered rabbits can't have babies. They tend to live longer and are calmer.

Meet the vet

Take your rabbit to the vet in a secure, well ventilated carrying box, with water and plenty of hay to nibble. The vet should be happy to advise you if you have any questions about your rabbit's diet, health or behaviour.

1 The vet might listen to your rabbit's heart and his breathing to make sure that they sound healthy. Pet your rabbit gently and speak to him softly to reassure him.

2 The vet will check your rabbit's ears, eyes, claws and coat. Ask her to show you how to do these checks and what to look out for, so that you can do them at home.

3 Dental problems are common in rabbits, so the vet will check his teeth. Ask her to show you how to check them so you can do it at home.

Vaccinations

Depending on where you live, your rabbit may need to be vaccinated against certain diseases. Ask the vet which diseases your rabbit needs protection against. Vaccinations are usually given by injection, and your rabbit will need to return to the vet for booster shots once a year.

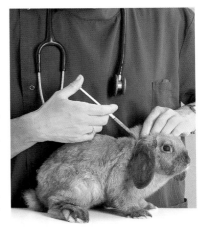

SIGNS OF ILLNESS

- Lack of appetite and loss of weight
- Runny nose and eyes, or sneezing
- Scratching and head-shaking
- Diarrhoea, lack of droppings, misshapen droppings or droppings with fur in
- Hunched position and lack of interest in life
- Dribbling, swollen face and difficulty eating
- Bald patches or sores

Call the vet

Rabbits can become seriously ill very suddenly. If you are worried in any way about your rabbit's health, take him straight to the vet. A sick rabbit will need lots of care and attention. He will need to be kept warm and calm and you may need to tempt him to eat.

WHERE TO LOOK

Baby and adult hamsters are available all year round from rescue centres, breeders and pet shops. Your local vet may be able to advise you about the best place to find a hamster.

Which hamster?

IF YOU DECIDE that you would like a pet hamster, you will need to find out where is the best place to get one and which type would suit you best. Your hamster will rely on you for everything – having a pet of your own is a big commitment. So take your time to look around until you find the perfect hamster.

Her eyes should be clear and bright.

Her coat should be clean, dry and smooth.

She should be nice and plump.

Her tail and bottom should be clean.

Healthy hamster

A healthy hamster is easy to spot. She will be active and alert, and clean and dry all over. Make sure that there is fresh bedding, food and water in her cage, and that any hamsters sharing with her look healthy, too.

Breeds and types

There are two main types of pet hamster – Syrians and Dwarfs. Syrians fight if they are kept in groups, so they must live alone. But Dwarf hamsters will live happily with other Dwarfs of the same type and sex.

Djungarian, or Russian, hamsters are usually easy to tame, and are the most popular Dwarf hamsters.

Have a hold

When you have found a hamster that you like, ask if you can hold it. Most hamsters can be tamed with regular handling, but it is best to choose one that does not panic or try to bite when it is picked up. You will know straight away when you have found the hamster that is right for you.

Syrian hamsters make great pets because they are usually friendly and easy to handle.

Never pick up a sleepy hamster – you might get a nasty bite.

At just 5 cm (2 in) from nose to tail, Roborovskys are the smallest Dwarf hamsters.

Siberian Dwarfs are also known as Winter Whites – their coats turn snow-white in the winter.

Syrian hamsters can be either long- or short-haired, and they come in all sorts of colours.

23

Hamsters can squeeze through surprisingly narrow spaces. If your hamster is small, a tank-style cage with solid sides is the safest choice.

Be prepared

IT IS IMPORTANT to make sure that you have everything ready for your hamster before you bring him home. You should be able to get all you need from your local pet shop. A cage with tunnels and different compartments to explore will keep your hamster busy.

Carrying box

Hamsters are expert escape-artists, so it is essential that you put your hamster somewhere safe while you clean out her cage or take her to see the vet. A purpose-built carrying box is ideal.

The carrying box must be well ventilated.

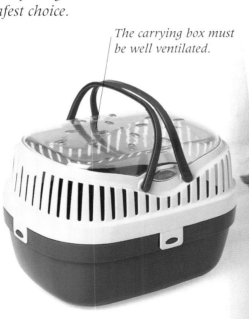

Cage comforts

Your hamster will need a layer of shavings in the bottom of his cage and some cosy bedding to nest in. Natural, unscented materials are best because they won't do your hamster any harm if he swallows some when he is making his bed.

Dust-free wood shavings

Corn husks

Plant fibre without dye

Preparing the cage

Once you have decided on a cage for your new hamster, you will need to find somewhere suitable to keep it. The cage should be placed above floor level and away from draughts, direct sunlight, radiators and cats. Make sure that the doors are easy to get to for cleaning out and feeding. Then make the cage inviting by adding bedding materials, toys and a nest box if there is not one built-in.

Check that any tunnels are large enough for your hamster to crawl through without getting stuck.

Hamster mix and bowl

Water bottle

FOOD AND WATER

Your hamster will need a heavy, chew-proof food bowl, some special hamster mix and a drip-feed bottle for water. Hamsters can be messy. Don't be surprised if yours fills his bowl with shavings and piles up bedding under his bottle so that it gets wet.

If your hamster's cage doesn't have fitted tunnels, give him an empty toilet roll to play in. He will enjoy nibbling it, too.

Toys and taming

HAMSTERS CAN MAKE entertaining pets. They will happily perform acrobatics in their cage while you watch, and are great fun to handle. When you first bring your new hamster home, allow her to settle for a couple of days. Then you can begin to make friends. Talk to her quietly and offer her bits of food. When your hamster is confident enough to eat from your hand, try to pick her up.

HAMSTER TOYS

Roller ball

Straw nest ball

Wood chew

Log tunnel

Hamsters love to climb and squeeze through holes and tunnels.

Hamsters use their excellent sense of smell to find their way around and locate food.

Preventing boredom

Hamsters are nocturnal (they sleep all day and are awake at night), so your hamster will be up and about when you are in bed. If she gets bored, she may try to escape from her cage. Keep her busy by providing toys and an exercise wheel. Choose a solid wheel so that she can't get her legs caught.

Playing safe

Hamsters can easily get lost behind furniture and under floorboards. If you don't have a hamster-proof area in your home, the safest way to let your hamster run around is inside a special exercise ball.

Handling

When you want to pick up your hamster, approach her carefully so you don't take her by surprise. Scoop her up gently using both hands and hold on to her firmly, without squeezing. Always hold her close over your lap or a flat surface in case she jumps or falls.

If you are nervous, ask someone experienced to hold your hamster while you pet him. You will soon feel more confident.

Making friends

If you handle your hamster every day, he will soon grow tame and begin to enjoy the attention. The best time to play with him is in the evening. If he is still asleep, open his cage and put a treat in his bowl. If he is ready to get up, he will smell the food and come to investigate.

Don't worry if your hamster's face looks fat – he has probably stuffed his cheek pouches with food.

Healthy diet

IT IS IMPORTANT that you provide your hamster with a varied, interesting and balanced diet because food will be the highlight of his day. Like his wild relatives, your hamster will spend most of his waking hours foraging for food and building up a hoard of his favourite things.

Balanced diet

The most important part of your hamster's diet is a good-quality hamster mix containing seeds, grains and pellets. She can also have a small piece of vegetable or fruit each day. A slice of cucumber or half a strawberry is plenty.

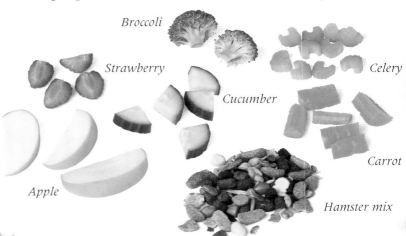

Broccoli

Strawberry

Cucumber

Celery

Carrot

Apple

Hamster mix

Evening meals

Feed your hamster every evening before you go to bed so that she can spend the night nibbling and hoarding any bits she wants to save for later. Put her food in a heavy bowl that doesn't easily tip up.

Your hamster will probably root through her bowl in search of her favourite bits.

FEEDING RULES

- Make sure that your hamster's drinking water is always clean and fresh.
- Wash and dry fruit and vegetables before giving them to your hamster.
- Remove any uneaten fresh food from the cage daily or it will go bad.
- Never feed your hamster large nuts or anything sticky or chewy.

Hand-feeding

Hamsters love their food. Hand-feeding treats to your hamster is a great way to tame him and win his affection. If you offer him a little treat every time you take him out of his cage, he will soon learn to look forward to being handled.

Unless your hamster is very relaxed, he will stuff food into his pouches to eat later.

If your hamster's pouches look full, put him back in his cage so he can empty them.

Yoghurt drops

Dried vegetables

Dried fruit

HEALTHY TREATS

All sorts of hamster treats are available in pet shops, but try to choose something that will not harm your hamster's teeth or make him fat. Dried fruit and vegetable pieces and special yoghurt drops are healthy choices, and most hamsters love them.

Clean hamster

YOUR HAMSTER WILL be living indoors with you, so it is especially important that you keep her cage clean and tidy. It will smell if it is not cleaned out often enough, and your hamster may get ill if she has to live in wet or dirty conditions. Your hamster will be quite good at keeping her own fur clean, but it is a good idea to groom her regularly, too.

After you have touched your hamster, she may groom herself to rearrange and clean her fur.

Daily grooming

Try to find time to groom your hamster every day. This will prevent long fur from getting matted, and will allow you to give your hamster a check-up. Look out for any patches of bald or sore skin and any unusual lumps or bumps on his body.

Hamster brushes are small and have soft bristles.

A small comb is ideal for a long-haired hamster.

Sit on the floor with a cushion or towel on your lap when you brush your hamster. Then, if he wriggles out of your hands, he will have a soft landing.

CLEANING TIPS

- If you don't have a special hamster brush, an old toothbrush will do just as well.
- Never used scented wood shavings as bedding for your hamster – it could make him ill or irritate his eyes and skin.
- Leave behind part of your hamster's stash of dry food when you clean him out. If you remove it all, he will feel insecure.

Cleaning the cage

You will need to clean out your hamster's cage at least once a week to prevent it smelling and to keep him healthy and comfortable. Choose a time when he is awake so that you don't disturb him. Put him in his carrying box so you know he is safe while you are cleaning his cage.

Make sure the cage is dry before you put your hamster back.

1 Start by scooping out all the dirty wood shavings and bedding from the bottom of your hamster's cage. Then empty out the old bedding from his nest box, keeping a clean bit to put back later.

2 Wipe the bottom of the cage with a damp cloth, then spray it with a pet-safe disinfectant. Wipe and spray the nest box and any wheels, ramps, tunnels and toys. Leave everything to dry for about half an hour.

3 Line the cage with fresh shavings and put fresh bedding material – plus the saved bit of old bedding – in the nest box. The old bedding will make your hamster feel at home when you put him back.

Wipe right into the corners of the cage.

Your hamster should live for up to two years but, as she gets older, she may become less active and spend more time sleeping.

Hamster health

IF YOU CARE for your hamster well, you will give him the best chance of a healthy life. Look out for signs of illness, and take him to the vet if you are worried. Hamsters and humans can catch some of the same germs. Always wash your hands before and after handling him and, if you are unwell, ask someone else to look after him until you are better.

Daily checks

Give your hamster a quick health check every day when you pick her up to groom or play with her. You will soon get to know her really well, and will notice straight away if something is wrong.

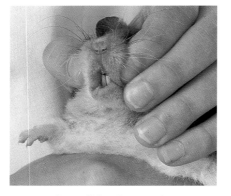

1 Gently pull back your hamster's lips. Her teeth should be short, sharp and yellowish. If they look long and are curling under, go to the vet to have them trimmed.

2 Check your hamster's claws. If they look long or are curled under, take her to the vet to have them clipped. Also make sure that her feet don't look sore or swollen.

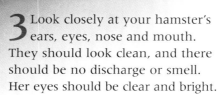

3 Look closely at your hamster's ears, eyes, nose and mouth. They should look clean, and there should be no discharge or smell. Her eyes should be clear and bright.

4 Your hamster's coat should be clean and dry. Check her all over, paying special attention to her bottom. If her bottom is wet or dirty, take her to the vet.

SIGNS OF ILLNESS

- Weight loss and lack of appetite
- Diarrhoea and wetness near tail
- Sneezing or breathing problems
- Discharge from eyes or nose
- Dribbling and difficulty eating
- Irritability and behaviour changes
- Skin sores or fur loss

First trip to the vet

Register with a small-animal vet before you bring home your new hamster, and take him to the vet for a check-up as soon as possible. The vet will look at your hamster carefully to make sure that he is healthy, and will confirm whether he is a boy or a girl.

The vet will show you how to pick up and hold your hamster correctly.

If you have any questions about caring for your hamster, ask the vet. She will be happy to advise you.

Choosing

THERE ARE LOTS of things to consider when you are choosing a guinea pig. Do you want one with a long, silky coat or a short, frizzy coat? Do you want to rescue a homeless guinea pig from a shelter or choose a pedigree baby from a breeder? Take your time and pick carefully. Your new guinea pig will need your care and attention for the whole of her life.

Your guinea pig will be happiest if she has the company of at least one other guinea pig. If possible, choose a pair from the same litter – they will become best friends.

His eyes should be clear and bright.

His coat should be clean, with no bald patches.

His nose and mouth should be clean and dry, with no sore areas.

His claws should not be too long.

Signs of good health

It is important to choose a healthy guinea pig. He should be clean all over, his eyes should be bright and he should be nice and plump. Choose a guinea pig that seems active, alert and friendly. One that is very quiet or shy may be unwell or hard to tame.

Colours and coats

The main differences between the various breeds of guinea pig are in their coats. Guinea pig coats come in all sorts of colours, patterns, lengths and styles. It won't be hard to find a guinea pig with that special appeal.

This Rex guinea pig has a short, frizzy coat. Rexes come in various colours. The Texel guinea pig has frizzy hair, too, but it is long-haired.

34

Finding your guinea pig

A rescue centre is a great place to start your search for a guinea pig. Many have a wide selection of baby and adult guinea pigs, all in need of loving homes. You could also contact a breeder in your area, visit a nearby pet shop or ask a local vet for advice. Wherever you decide to go, don't be afraid to ask questions. Ask to hold the guinea pig you choose before making your final decision. The owner should be happy to help you.

CHOOSING CHECK LIST

- Is the guinea pig alert and active?
- Does he seem curious and interested in you?
- Has he been kept in good conditions, with clean bedding and fresh food and water?
- Is his coat in good condition?
- Are his eyes, nose, ears, mouth and bottom clean?
- Does he like being handled?
- Do the other guinea pigs he has been living with look healthy?

This Abyssinian cross has a rough, medium-length coat. His hair forms peaks, or rosettes, all over his body.

The Sheltie has long, straight, smooth hair, which can grow up to 60 cm (24 in) long. Shelties need careful, regular grooming and trimming.

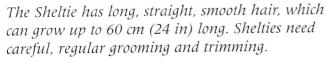

Satin guinea pigs have silky, fine coats. They are available in all colours, and can be short-haired or long-haired.

BASIC ESSENTIALS

Carrying box with removable lid

Wood-based litter and tray

Dust-free wood shavings

Dust-free hay

Dust-free straw

Cleaning materials

Grooming kit

Food and bowl *Water bottle*

What you need

YOUR NEW GUINEA pig will need a comfortable, spacious hutch, a run to exercise in and a supply of bedding material and food. You will also need to get a carrying box so that you can bring him home safely, a grooming kit and equipment for keeping his hutch, bowl and water bottle clean. Make sure you have prepared the essentials before bringing your guinea pig home.

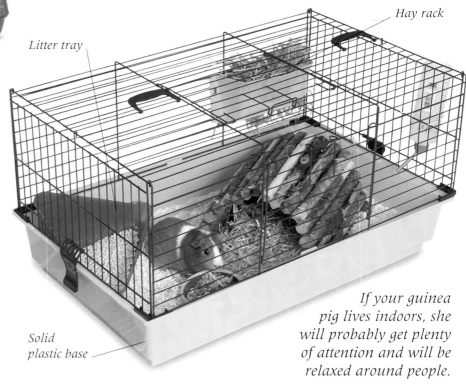

Hay rack

Litter tray

Solid plastic base

If your guinea pig lives indoors, she will probably get plenty of attention and will be relaxed around people.

Indoor hutch

If you want to keep your guinea pig indoors, she will need a special hutch. Choose the largest one you have room for, and make sure that it has a solid base, is well ventilated and has somewhere for your guinea pig to hide away and sleep. A hutch with a wire floor could make your guinea pig's feet sore, so choose one with a solid base and cover it with a layer of bedding.

Outdoor hutch

If you provide your guinea pig with a weather-proof hutch, he can live outside for most of the year. The hutch should be at least 100 cm (40 in) square and 50 cm (20 in) tall. It should have an enclosed sleeping compartment and a wire door so he can see out. In spells of very hot or cold weather, your guinea pig will need to be kept indoors.

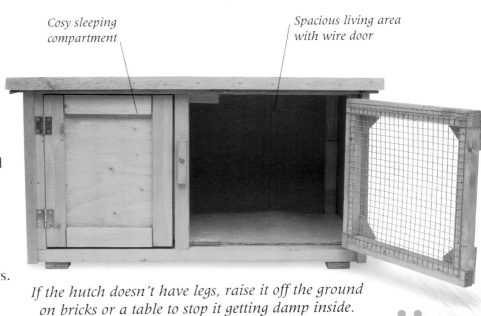

Cosy sleeping compartment

Spacious living area with wire door

If the hutch doesn't have legs, raise it off the ground on bricks or a table to stop it getting damp inside.

Exercise run

Whether your guinea pig lives inside or outside, she will need an outdoor run where she can graze and exercise. The more room she has to explore and root around in the grass, the happier she will be. The enclosure should have a sheltered area for protection from hot sun and rain and a place for your guinea pig to hide. It should be portable so it can be moved to a fresh patch of grass each day.

Make sure that the enclosure is safe from cats, dogs and other predators.

Friends for life

YOUR GUINEA PIG pig will need time to get used to her new home. Put her in her hutch and make sure she has plenty of food and water. Then leave her in peace for the rest of the day. When she seems settled, you can start to make friends. Sit by her hutch and talk gently to her without trying to pick her up. She will soon get to know you, and will let you pet and handle her without a struggle.

Handle with care

Guinea pigs can be hard to catch, but it is important to be patient and gentle. You could hurt your guinea pig if you grab him. Approach him from the front so he can see you coming, and put one hand around his chest and shoulders. Put your other hand under his bottom and pick him up. Always use two hands, and hold him close to your body.

Never let your guinea pig fall. Even a small drop could do serious damage.

Meet the family

When your new guinea pig has settled in, you can start to introduce him to your family and friends. Make sure they know how to handle him properly, and take care not to overwhelm him. The more people he meets, the tamer he will become, but too many introductions in one day might make him nervous.

Don't introduce your guinea pig to a cat – the results could be fatal.

When a pair of guinea pigs have bonded, they will follow each other around and cuddle up to rest.

Other guinea pigs

If you already have a guinea pig at home, ask your vet for advice before introducing your new guinea pig. If they are both males, they may fight. And if you have a male and a female, you are likely to end up with lots of baby guinea pigs.

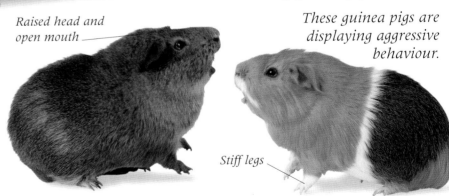

Raised head and open mouth

These guinea pigs are displaying aggressive behaviour.

Stiff legs

GUINEA PIG TALK

- Your guinea pig may squeal with excitement when she sees you, especially if you are bringing food.
- Chattering and hissing are signs of aggression.
- Your guinea pig may grunt and squeak at her friends – it is a sign of happiness.
- If your guinea pig "coos" when you are petting her, don't stop – she's loving it!

Body language

As well as learning to understand the sounds your guinea pig makes, you can also tell a lot from watching her body language. If she is frightened she will freeze; if she feels relaxed she will snuggle down with her tummy on the floor; and if she is angry she will raise her head and arch her back.

Make sure your guinea pig can reach his water easily.

The right diet

GUINEA PIGS NEED a diet rich in certain nutrients, especially vitamin C. You can buy pellets that contain all your guinea pig needs, but you should supplement his diet with fresh fruit and vegetables. He will also need a constant supply of hay to nibble, and grazing time whenever possible.

Bottled water

Make sure that your guinea pig has a supply of fresh water at all times. A drip-feed bottle is better than a bowl because your guinea pig won't be able to knock it over or get food and bedding in it.

Guinea pig pellets

Pellets

Good quality guinea pig pellets are the most important part of your guinea pig's diet. Weigh him and check the packet to find out how much he needs each day. Feed him half in the morning and half in the evening so he always has something to eat. Store the pellets in an airtight box to keep them fresh.

Cucumber

Guinea pigs get a lot of the water they need from juicy fruit and vegetables.

Strawberry

Orange

Carrot

Apple

Celery

Broccoli

Cauliflower

Dark green leafy vegetables are very high in vitamin C.

Cabbage

Dried vegetables

Vegetable biscuits

Dried fruit

TREATS

Even if your guinea pig is very shy at first, he will probably find the courage to accept a tasty titbit from your hand. Offering healthy treats like dried fruit and vegetables is a good way to gain your guinea pig's trust.

Supplements

Fresh fruit and vegetables contain vitamin C, and guinea pigs love them. Feed your guinea pig a large handful of mixed fruit and vegetables every day to add variety to her diet. You will soon discover which are her favourites and which she is less interested in.

Regular routine

Guinea pigs are creatures of habit,
so feed your guinea pig at around the
same times every day. She will quickly
learn when to expect you, and will greet
you with excited squeaks when she sees
you coming. Try to avoid drastic changes
to your feeding routine – they could
cause your guinea pig to stop eating.

(!)

Don't feed your
guinea pig rabbit
food. It doesn't
contain the right
nutrients, and she
may become ill.

FEEDING RULES

- Wash and dry all fruit
  and vegetables before
  feeding them to your
  guinea pig.

- Throw away any uneaten
  pellets every day.

- Make changes to your
  guinea pig's diet slowly.
  Sudden changes may
  upset her tummy.

- Wash, rinse and dry her
  bowl and bottle daily.

Cleaning up

Guinea pigs groom themselves
with their teeth and front paws.
They sometimes get so carried
away that they topple over.

IT IS ESSENTIAL to your guinea pig's health that
you keep her coat and hutch clean and dry at all
times. You will need to groom her regularly, bath
her from time to time and attend to her hutch
daily. Set aside at least 20 minutes every day
for keeping your guinea pig and her
home clean and tidy.

The right kit

Guinea pigs have delicate skin, so it
is important that you choose the right
grooming tools. A small, soft brush and
a wide-toothed comb are ideal. If your
guinea pig is long-haired, you may
need to ask an adult to help you trim
her coat from time to time.

Brush
and comb

Long-haired guinea pigs
need grooming every day,
but short-haired guinea
pigs can be groomed weekly.

Bathing

If your guinea pig's coat gets
dirty or greasy, you will need
to bath her. Always ask an
adult to help you. You will
need a bowl of luke-warm
water, some small-animal
shampoo and a towel. Wet
and lather your guinea
pig's coat, avoiding her
eyes and ears, then
rinse and dry
her thoroughly.

How to groom

Most guinea pigs enjoy being
groomed, and it is a good way to
bond with your pet. Brush your
guinea pig gently all over in the
direction of the hair growth, taking
great care near her eyes and ears.

Cleaning the hutch

Your guinea pig's hutch will need a full clean-out at least once a week, more often if she plays with her water bottle and makes her bedding material wet. You will also need to replace dirty bedding and litter and replenish her hay once every day.

CLEANING AN INDOOR HUTCH

An indoor hutch may need cleaning out more often than an outdoor one because any smell will be more noticeable. Put newspaper under her hutch to catch any stray hay or wood shavings. When you clean the hutch, roll up the newspaper, throw it away and replace it.

1 Put your guinea pig in her run or carrying box, and then remove all the dirty bedding and litter from her hutch. Clean right into the corners.

2 About once a month, use a pet-safe disinfectant and a stiff brush to clean the empty hutch and litter tray. Allow everything to dry out completely.

3 Put a fresh layer of wood shavings on the floor of the hutch and a large pile of hay or straw in the nest area. Fill the litter tray with clean litter.

4 When you have finished cleaning, you can return your guinea pig to her hutch. Give her some food and water, then leave her for a while to rearrange her bedding and settle back in.

Your guinea pig may get ill if she has to live in damp or dirty conditions.

A happy life

IF YOUR GUINEA pig has enough living and exercise space, lots of human and guinea pig company and some simple accessories to keep him occupied in his hutch and run, he should live a full and happy life. If you spend lots of time with him, you will soon get to know him, and will notice immediately if there is something wrong.

Guinea pigs love to root around in hay and long grass. A large pile of hay will also give him a cosy place to hide and something to nibble on.

Playmates

Guinea pigs are very sociable animals, so it is kindest to keep at least two together. A bonded pair will keep each other company when you are not around and will be great fun to watch as they scuttle from place to place together squeaking and grunting.

Your guinea pig's true character will emerge if she has a friend to play with.

Outdoor fun

As long as the weather isn't very wet or cold, and you are around to keep an eye on her, your guinea pig will be happy to spend most of the day in her exercise run. Give her something new to explore every now and then to prevent her from getting bored.

A piece of ceramic piping and some large stones make a great guinea pig playground.

INDOOR SAFETY

- Make sure there are no gaps or holes that your guinea pig could disappear through.
- Move or protect any electric cables.
- Be careful where you tread and sit.

You and your guinea pig

The more time you spend with your guinea pig, the happier he will be. Chat to him and stroke him as much as you can. When the weather isn't suitable for him to play outside, bring him indoors for a cuddle, a change of scenery and a run-around.

Health matters

TAKE YOUR NEW guinea pig to a small-animal vet for a health check as soon as you can. The vet will make sure that she is fit and well, and will answer any questions you have about her care. Regular health checks, good housing and a balanced diet will be essential to your guinea pig's health throughout her life. She will also need some special care when she is a baby and when she reaches old age.

Baby guinea pigs look like miniature adults, but need their mother's care for the first six weeks of life.

1 The vet may listen to your guinea pig's heart and breathing to make sure they sound normal.

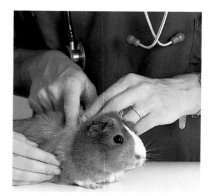

2 She will check your guinea pig's coat and skin for any signs of lice or mites, and will make sure that she is not too fat or too thin.

First check-up

The vet will confirm whether your guinea pig is a boy or a girl, and will check her thoroughly all over. If you have more than one guinea pig, she will advise you about neutering to prevent unwanted babies. Neutered guinea pigs tend to live longer.

3 She will check your guinea pig's ears, eyes, mouth and nose for any signs of infection or other problems.

Health routine

Ask the vet to show you how to carry out basic health checks and what to look for. If you check your guinea pig regularly, you will be aware early on of any problems. Sit down on the floor with your guinea pig, and make sure that she is calm before carrying out the checks. If you are worried about your guinea pig's health, take her straight to the vet.

Drooping eyelids shouldn't be a problem, as long as there is no discharge.

Stiff joints can cause discomfort.

Swollen feet can occur in old age.

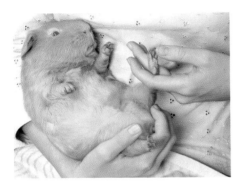

1 Your guinea pig's claws will need trimming from time to time. Check them every few days to make sure they don't look too long or curled under. Ask the vet to show you how to trim them.

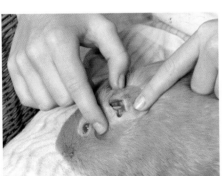

2 Fold back her ears and look inside. If you see any dirt or discharge, wipe it away with a piece of damp cotton wool. Take your guinea pig to the vet if the discharge comes back or if it is smelly.

3 Your guinea pig's teeth will keep growing all her life, and may occasionally need trimming by the vet. Check for overgrown teeth by gently lifting her upper lips and pulling down her lower lips.

Old age

A well cared-for guinea pig can live for about seven years. As your guinea pig gets older, he will need special care. He may become more sensitive to hot and cold weather, and is likely to be less active. Take him to the vet if he seems to be in any pain or if he is unable to eat, drink or move about.

SIGNS OF ILLNESS

- Refusal to eat or loss of weight
- Scratching and bald patches or sores
- Refusal to move, stiff movement or swollen joints
- Diarrhoea or lack of droppings
- Breathing problems or discharge from the nose or eyes
- Swollen or dirty bottom

Index

ACKNOWLEDGEMENTS

BOOKWORK LTD WOULD LIKE TO THANK:
Gudrun Tingle from Cotswold Guinea Pig Rescue for various guinea pigs and advice; Debbie Pollard from Debbie's Lops for baby rabbits; Pets at Home for props; and the following pets and their owners: Max and Mrs Snuffles the hamsters; Manny, Hope and Bonnie the rabbits; and Margot the guinea pig.

MODELS

Kayleigh Adams, Adam Blackledge, Oliver Curwen, Verity Curwen, William Curwen, Howard Hall, Ellie Morgan, Joseph Morgan, Sasha Plank, Harvey Skelton, Jack Skelton, Jess Skelton, Eleanor Teague, Megan Teague and Rosemary Teague